RSPB

first book of
mammals

Anita Ganeri and David Chandler

Published 2011 by A&C Black Publishers Limited
36 Soho Square, London W1D 3QY
www.acblack.com

ISBN: 978-1-4081-3716-1

Printed and bound in China by WKT.

A&C Black uses paper produced from elemental
chlorine-free pulp, harvested from managed
sustainable forests.

Contents

Introduction   5

Badger   6
Pipistrelle bat   7
Noctule bat   8
Long-eared bat   9
Red deer   10
Fallow deer   11
Roe deer   12
Red fox   13
Brown hare   14
Mountain hare   15
Rabbit   16
Hedgehog   17
Mole   18
House mouse   19
Wood mouse   20
Harvest mouse   21
Brown rat   22
Field vole   23
Bank vole   24

Water vole	25
Common shrew	26
Water shrew	27
Common dormouse	28
Otter	29
Pine marten	30
Grey squirrel	31
Red squirrel	32
Stoat	33
Weasel	34
Wildcat	35
Grey seal	36
Common seal	37
Common porpoise	38
Bottle-nosed dolphin	39
Minke whale	40
Useful words	41
Spotter's guide	42-47
Find out more	48

Mammals

Mammals are everywhere! Perhaps you have seen a rabbit, a grey squirrel or a hedgehog?

This book tells you about these mammals and lots of other ones. Stay up late in the summer and you might see bats – these are mammals that fly! You could go on a special boat trip to see seals. Or you might be lucky and see a stoat run across the road.

At the back of this book is a Spotter's Guide to help you remember the mammals you spot. You could also write down the mammals you see, or draw them.

Turn the page to find out all about mammals!

Badger

Badgers come out at night. They are very shy of people. They live underground in woods and hedges. Their home is called a sett. They eat worms, minibeasts, small mammals, birds' eggs, seeds and fruit.

About the size of a medium-sized dog

Black fur

Short legs

Big claws to dig with

Badgers sometimes come into people's gardens.

Pipistrelle bat

Pipistrelle bats are the bats you are most likely to see. Look for them on summer evenings as it gets dark. They fly fast, twisting and turning. In the day, pipistrelles roost in bat boxes, trees and buildings.

When it closes its wings, a pipistrelle is so small that it can fit into a matchbox.

Ears

Wings

Small, furry body

They eat midges and other small insects.

Noctule bat

These are some of the biggest bats in Britain. In the evenings, they fly fast high above the trees. Watch them dive down suddenly to catch their dinner.

Baby noctule bats can fly when they are four weeks old.

Wings

Ears

Most noctules sleep in holes in trees.

Long-eared bat

This bat has very big ears. Its ears are almost as long as its body. It flies very slowly. It uses its eyes and ears to find insects to eat.

When it sleeps, a long-eared bat puts its ears under its wings.

Very long ears

It flies low over water to drink.

Big eyes for a bat

Red deer

Red deer are the biggest deer in Britain. They live in woods, and on moors and mountains. Only the males have antlers. They grow new ones every year.

Male red deer roar in autumn to show how strong they are.

Spiky antlers

Brown fur, redder in summer.

Sometimes males fight each other.

Fallow deer

Fallow deer are smaller than red deer. They can be brown, black or white. Some have spots. You can see them in woods and grassy areas.

Fallow deer eat grass, nuts, berries, leaves and bark.

Antlers. Not on young males or females.

Long tail. Some deer have black or brown stripe on tail

Brown with white spots. Greyer in winter.

Usually fallow deer have one fawn (baby deer) in a year.

Roe deer

Roe deer live in woods and are about the size of big dogs. If you see one, stay still. It will only notice you if you move. Its summer coat is pale brown to red-brown. In winter, it is darker brown or grey.

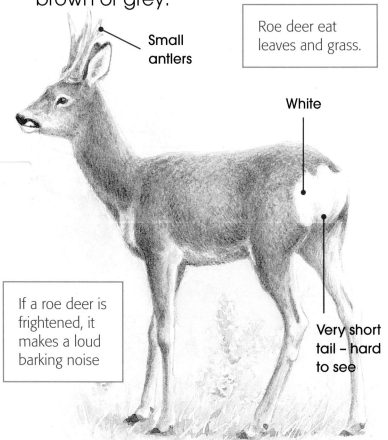

Small antlers

Roe deer eat leaves and grass.

White

If a roe deer is frightened, it makes a loud barking noise

Very short tail – hard to see

Red fox

Red foxes come out at night. They dig a hole in the ground to live in called an 'earth'. Sometimes they use an old badgers' sett or rabbits' burrow instead.

Foxes eat insects, worms, birds, mice and rabbits. Some look through rubbish for food.

Pointed ears

A fox hides spare food so that it can eat it later.

White fur

Red-brown fur

Bushy tail. Sometimes has a white tip

A male is called a dog fox and a female is called a vixen.

Brown hare

Brown hares are bigger than rabbits. They have longer legs and long ears with black tips. They can run very fast. Look for them on flat grassy areas and farmland.

They sleep in scraped-out dips in the ground. These are called 'forms'.

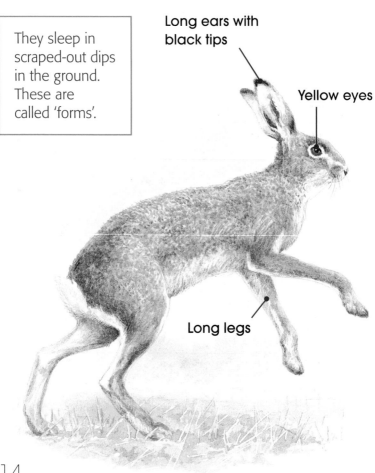

Long ears with black tips

Yellow eyes

Long legs

Mountain hare

In summer, a mountain hare has brown fur. In winter, its fur is white. This helps to hide it in the snow. However, its tail is white all year round.

Mountain hares live on moors and mountains. They come out at night.

Baby hares are called leverets.

Summer coat

Winter coat

White tail

Rabbit

It is easy to get rabbits and hares mixed up. Rabbits are smaller than hares. They have shorter ears with no black on the tips.

No black tip

Rabbits live in burrows. The females do most of the digging.

Long ears

Brown-grey fur

White

If they are scared, rabbits thump the ground with their back legs. This tells other rabbits to watch out.

Hedgehog

You can see hedgehogs in gardens and parks. They come out at night and sleep through the winter. Hedgehogs eat slugs, snails, worms, insects and birds' eggs. They can swim and climb.

A hedgehog can curl up into a spiky ball to protect itself.

Lots of prickles

Furry face

Long snout

Young hedgehogs are called hoglets.

Mole

It is very hard to see moles. They spend nearly all their lives underground. They use their big front feet for digging tunnels. Moles have tiny eyes but are not blind.

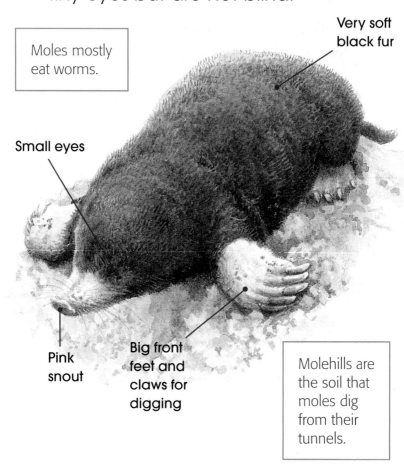

Moles mostly eat worms.

Very soft black fur

Small eyes

Pink snout

Big front feet and claws for digging

Molehills are the soil that moles dig from their tunnels.

House mouse

If you see a mouse in your house it is probably a house mouse. House mice come out at night. They eat seeds and minibeasts, but will also eat almost anything they can find!

House mice don't just live in buildings. Some live on rubbish tips and in hedges.

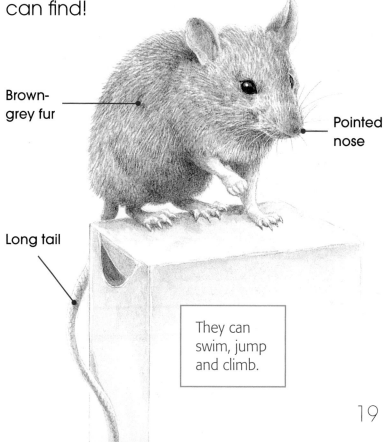

Brown-grey fur

Pointed nose

Long tail

They can swim, jump and climb.

19

Wood mouse

A wood mouse has bigger eyes and ears than a house mouse. Its tail is longer too. It eats acorns and other seeds, berries, buds and minibeasts.

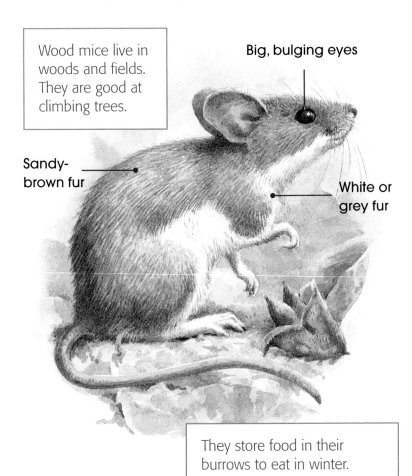

Wood mice live in woods and fields. They are good at climbing trees.

Big, bulging eyes

Sandy-brown fur

White or grey fur

They store food in their burrows to eat in winter.

Harvest mouse

This is the smallest mouse in Britain. It has a long tail. It uses this tail to help it climb in long grass. A harvest mouse is very hard to see, but you might find its nest. The nest is round and made from grass.

A harvest mouse can wind its long tail around a stalk of grass.

Orangey-brown fur

White fur

Long tail

Harvest mice eat seeds, berries and minibeasts.

Brown rat

A brown rat is much bigger than a mouse. It is good at digging and jumping. It can swim too. Brown rats live on farms, in towns and in sewers.

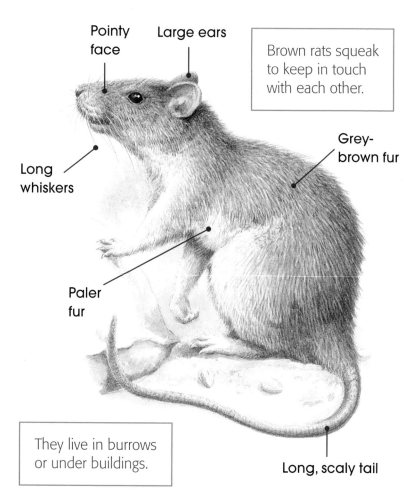

Pointy face

Large ears

Brown rats squeak to keep in touch with each other.

Long whiskers

Grey-brown fur

Paler fur

They live in burrows or under buildings.

Long, scaly tail

Field vole

Field voles are very common but they are hard to spot. They scurry about in long grass. They can stay hidden there. Field voles eat bark, grass and other plants.

Field voles can find their food by smelling it.

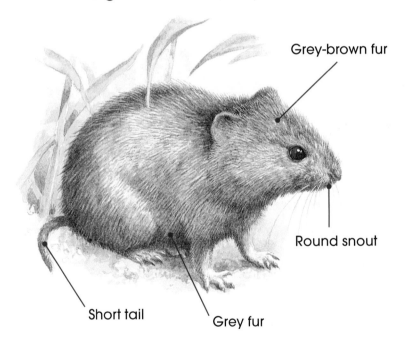

Grey-brown fur

Round snout

Short tail

Grey fur

Field voles fight with their neighbours in the grass.

Bank vole

It is easy to get a field vole and a bank vole mixed up. A bank vole has red-brown fur. Its fur looks smoother than a field vole's. It also has a longer tail. It lives in woods and hedges.

Bank voles nest in tunnels underground.

They eat leaves, fruit, seeds and minibeasts.

Red-brown fur

Grey fur

They leave patches of wee to tell other bank voles they are there.

Water vole

Look out for water voles swimming in rivers, canals, streams and lakes. Water voles are dark brown or black. They dig tunnels in the riverbanks to live in.

Most water voles have secret exit tunnels underwater.

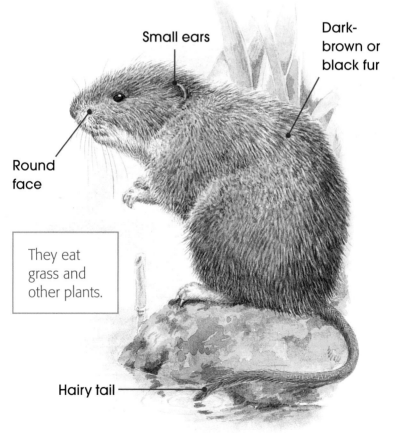

Small ears

Dark-brown or black fur

Round face

They eat grass and other plants.

Hairy tail

Common shrew

Look out for a shrew's long, pointed nose. Common shrews eat insects, worms and other minibeasts. Shrews have to eat almost non-stop. They will die if they don't eat every three or four hours.

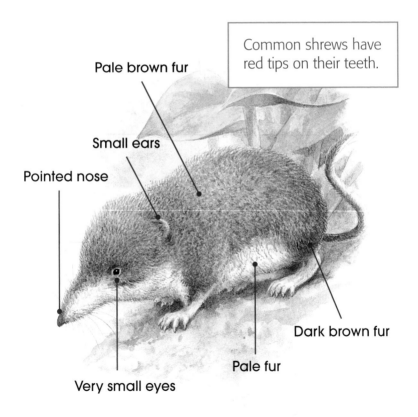

Pale brown fur

Common shrews have red tips on their teeth.

Small ears

Pointed nose

Dark brown fur

Pale fur

Very small eyes

Water shrew

A water shrew is a great swimmer and can dive underwater. It eats minibeasts, little fish, tadpoles and frogs. It catches its food in the water and on land.

Water shrews have poison in their spit.

Black fur

Silvery hairs

They trap air bubbles in their fur. This helps them to float.

Pale fur

Silvery hairs

27

Common dormouse

Dormice come out at night. They live in trees and climb along branches looking for food. Dormice eat fruit and nuts. They make nests in holes in branches and old birds' nests.

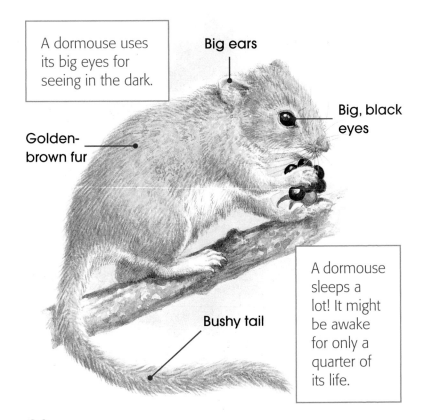

A dormouse uses its big eyes for seeing in the dark.

Big ears

Big, black eyes

Golden-brown fur

A dormouse sleeps a lot! It might be awake for only a quarter of its life.

Bushy tail

Otter

Otters live near rivers and lakes and by the sea. They have webbed feet to help them swim. They keep most of their body underwater as they swim.

An otter has thick, oily fur that is warm and waterproof.

Otters use their poo to tell other otters they live there.

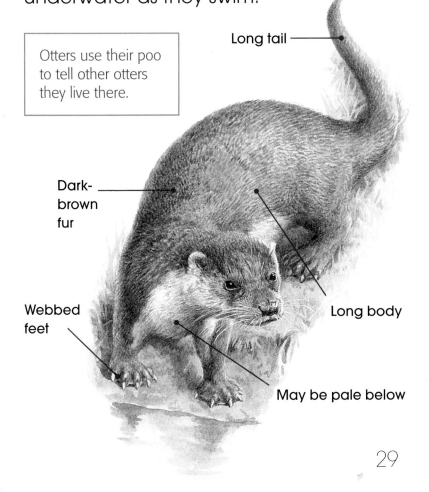

Long tail

Dark-brown fur

Webbed feet

Long body

May be pale below

Pine martin

Pine martens live in forests. They are about the size of a cat. Pine martens are great at climbing trees. They eat voles, squirrels, frogs, birds, insects, fruit and dead animals.

Pine martens raid bumblebee nests to get at the honey inside them.

Creamy-yellow fur

Dark-brown fur

Bushy tail

Grey squirrel

Grey squirrels are very easy to see. Look for them in parks, gardens and woods. They scamper across the ground and up trees. Grey squirrels eat nuts, seeds, and other bits of plants. Sometimes they take food from birdfeeders.

In autumn, grey squirrels store food to eat in winter.

A grey squirrel's nest is a ball of leaves, twigs and grass. It is called a drey.

Long, bushy tail

Grey fur

Red squirrel

Red squirrels are only found in a few places in Britain. They live in big forests. Sometimes they come into gardens. Pine seeds are one of their favourite foods. They also eat bark, berries and other seeds.

Red squirrels can swim well.

Bushy tail

Orangey fur

A red squirrel holds a pine cone in its paws and bites it to get at the seeds.

Stoat

You might see a stoat running across the road. Look for the black tip on its tail. Stoats are fierce hunters. They eat rabbits, small mammals and birds. In some places, stoats turn white in winter to hide themselves in the snow.

Stoats are very good climbers.

A stoat's white winter coat is called 'ermine'. But it still has its black tail-tip.

White fur

Brown fur

Black tip

Weasel

A weasel is much smaller than a stoat. Its tail is shorter and does not have a black tip. A weasel's favourite food is voles and mice. It is slim enough to chase these animals right into their burrows.

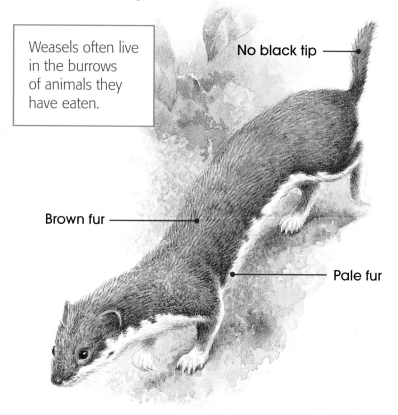

Weasels often live in the burrows of animals they have eaten.

No black tip

Brown fur

Pale fur

Wildcat

Wildcats are very hard to see. They live on the edges of some forests in Scotland. Dawn and dusk are the best times to see them. They look like big pet tabby cats.

Wildcats hunt at night. In the day, they rest in their dens.

Stripes

Thick tail

They hunt small mammals, rabbits, hares and birds. Sometimes they eat fish!

Grey seal

Sometimes you can see grey seals lying on rocks or beaches by the sea. They have a thick layer of fat under their skin to keep them warm. Grey seals eat fish.

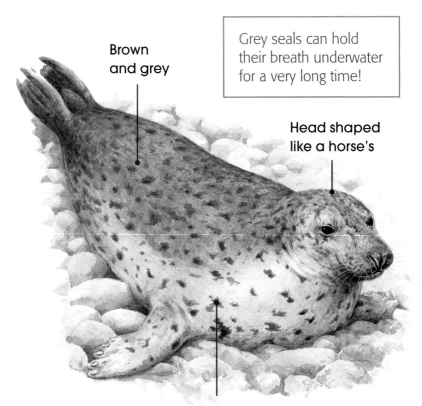

Brown and grey

Grey seals can hold their breath underwater for a very long time!

Head shaped like a horse's

May have blotches

Common seal

To tell a common seal from a grey seal look at its head shape. A common seal has a head like a dog, and a grey seal has a head like a horse.

Common seals eat fish, squid and shrimps.

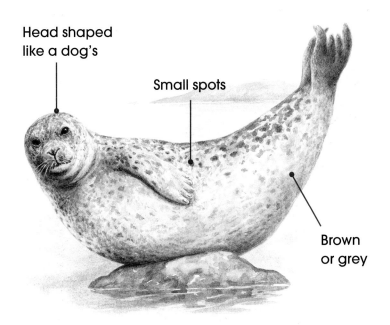

Head shaped like a dog's

Small spots

Brown or grey

Baby common seals (pups) can swim when they are a few hours old.

Common porpoise

A common porpoise is about as long as a grown-up. Look for these mammals in the sea and in river mouths near the sea. They eat fish, squid, cuttlefish and shrimps.

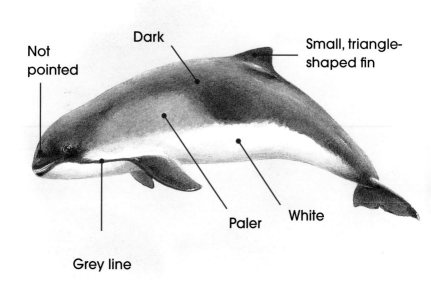

Dark

Small, triangle-shaped fin

Not pointed

Paler

White

Grey line

Small groups of common porpoises swim near the coast.

Bottle-nosed dolphin

A bottle-nosed dolphin gets its name from the shape of its beak. It breathes through a

A bottle-nosed dolphin moves its tail up and down to swim.

blowhole on top of its head. It lives in most of the seas around the world.

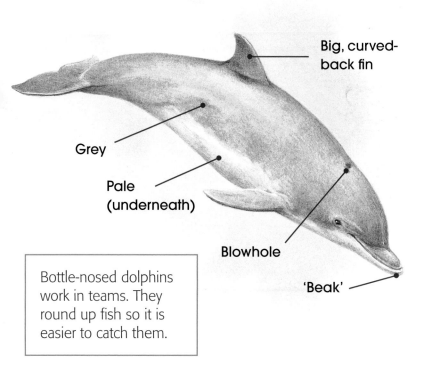

Big, curved-back fin

Grey

Pale (underneath)

Blowhole

'Beak'

Bottle-nosed dolphins work in teams. They round up fish so it is easier to catch them.

Minke whale

A minke whale is as long as a school coach, but it is actually quite small for a whale. Instead of teeth, it has something called baleen, which looks like a comb.
It uses this to sift food out of the water.

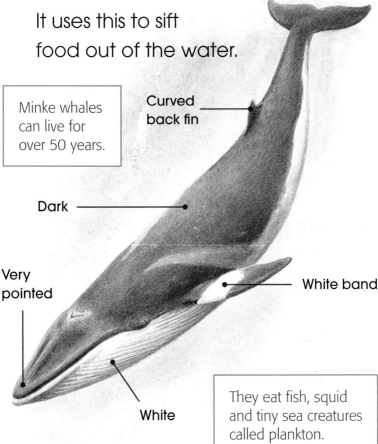

Minke whales can live for over 50 years.

Curved back fin

Dark

Very pointed

White band

White

They eat fish, squid and tiny sea creatures called plankton.

Useful words

bat boxes small boxes for bats to live in

blotches different-coloured marks on the skin

blowhole a hole for breathing, on the top of the head of a dolphin or whale

fin the parts of a fish that are like paddles to help steer it in the water

midges small flies that often move in swarms near ponds and lakes

moors large, open pieces of land, often covered with heather

scurry run about

snout a long nose and mouth

webbed feet where the toes are joined by thin flaps of skin to help the animal swim

Spotter's guide

How many of these
mammals have you
seen? Tick them
when you spot them.

☐ Badger
page 6

☐ Pipistrelle bat
page 7

☐ Noctule bat
page 8

☐ Long-eared bat
page 9

☐ Red deer
page 10

Fallow deer
page 11

Roe deer
page 12

Red fox
page 13

Brown hare
page 14

Mountain hare
page 15

Rabbit
page 16

Hedgehog
page 17

Mole
page 18

House mouse
page 19

Wood mouse
page 20

Harvest mouse
page 21

Brown rat
page 22

Field vole
page 23

Bank vole
page 24

Water vole
page 25

Common shrew
page 26

Water shrew
page 27

Common
dormouse
page 28

Otter
page 29

Pine marten
page 30

Grey squirrel
page 31

Red squirrel
page 32

Stoat
page 33

Weasel
page 34

Wildcat
page 35

Grey seal
page 36

Common seal
page 37

Common porpoise
page 38

Bottle-nosed
dolphin
page 39

Minke whale
page 40

Find out more

If you have enjoyed this book and would like to find out more about mammals and other wildlife, you might like RSPB Wildlife Explorers.

Visit www.rspb.org.uk/youth to find lots of things to make and do, and to play brilliant wildlife games.